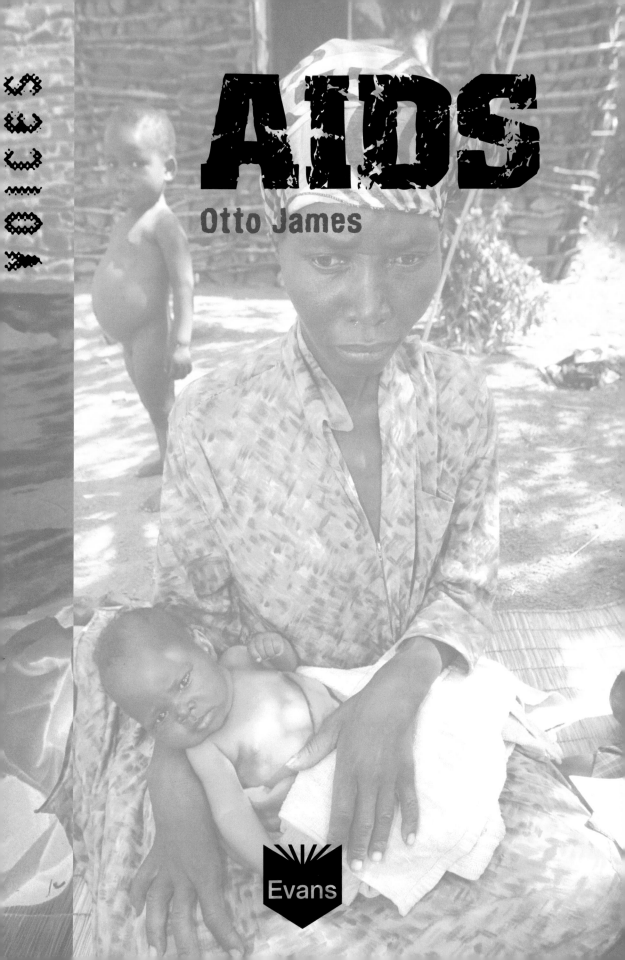

AIDS

Otto James

Evans

TITLES IN THE VOICES SERIES:

AIDS • CHILD LABOUR • DRUGS ON THE STREET • GANGS

HUNGER • POVERTY • RACE HATE • RELIGIOUS EXTREMISM

VIOLENCE • VIOLENCE ON THE SCREEN • WAR

Published by Evans Brothers Limited
2A Portman Mansions
Chiltern Street
London W1U 6NR

First published 2009
© copyright Evans Brothers 2009

VISIT OUR WEBSITE
Evans
www.evansbooks.co.uk

Produced for Evans Brothers Limited by
Monkey Puzzle Media Ltd
Little Manor Farm, The Street
Brundish, Woodbridge
Suffolk IP13 8BL, UK

The right of Otto James to be identified as the author of this Work has been asserted by him in accordance with the Copyright, Designs and Patents Act 1988.

British Library Cataloguing in Publication Data
James, Otto
AIDS. – (Voices)
1. AIDS (Disease) – Juvenile literature
I. Title
362.1'969792

ISBN-13: 978 0 237 53717 3

Editor: Susie Brooks
Designer: Mayer Media Ltd
Picture research: Susie Brooks and Lynda Lines
Graphs and charts: Martin Darlison, Encompass Graphics

Picture acknowledgements
Photographs were kindly supplied by the following:
Alamy 15 (Doug Menuez), 33 (Directphoto.org); Corbis 9 (Steve Nagy/Design Pics), 16 (Jean Louis Atlan/Sygma), 38 (Shayne Robinson), 39 (Gideon Mendel); Getty Images 1 (AFP), 8, 10 (AFP), 13 (AFP), 18 (Time & Life Pictures), 23 (AFP), 24 (National Geographic), 26 (AFP), 27 (AFP), 28 (Robert Daly), 30, 36 (AFP), 40, 41, 42–43; Panos Pictures 6 (Mark Henley), 7 (Chris Stowers), 25 (Giacomo Pirozzi), 29 (Qilai Shen), 35 (Sven Torfinn), 37 (Chris de Bode), 45 (Qilai Shen); Reuters front cover (Sukree Sukplang); Rex Features 12 (Mikko Stig), 14 (Sipa), 32 (Tony Larkin); Topfoto.co.uk 20–21 (The Image Works), 31 (The Image Works).

Cover picture: A six-year-old boy who contracted AIDS in his mother's womb stands in his bed at a children's home in Bangkok, Thailand.

CONTENTS

WHAT IS HIV/AIDS?

AIDS stands for Acquired Immune Deficiency Syndrome. AIDS is a killer disease, and there is no cure. In 2007, roughly 33 million people were living with AIDS. That same year, over 2 million people died of the disease.

HIV and AIDS

AIDS is linked to a virus called HIV. The HIV virus lives inside people's bodies, and makes it hard for them to fight off diseases. To someone with HIV, even an ordinary cold can be a serious illness – as Jane from Edinburgh, Scotland explains:

❝ My body can't fight off illnesses alone, so every day I have to take special drugs. Without them, even a cold or flu could turn to pneumonia, – and that can be a killer if you have AIDS. ❞

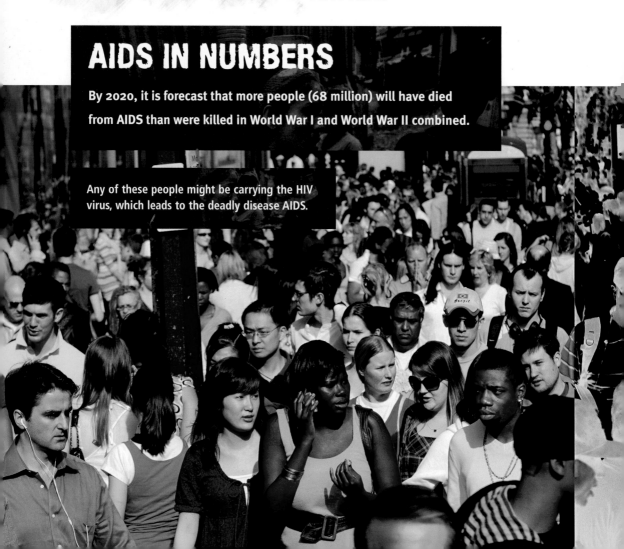

AIDS IN NUMBERS

By 2020, it is forecast that more people (68 million) will have died from AIDS than were killed in World War I and World War II combined.

Any of these people might be carrying the HIV virus, which leads to the deadly disease AIDS.

Developing AIDS

There is no cure for HIV. As the virus grows stronger inside the body, it begins to have more serious effects. Eventually it becomes full-blown AIDS. The illness has a terrible end, as the mother of one sufferer describes:

❝ His skin was an even darker yellow-green than it had been the first day I arrived, and he was laying against the white hospital sheets, gasping for breath. I went to his bedside, took his hand, hugged him, and softly called his name. He didn't respond. It was apparent he didn't even know I was there. ❞

This girl in Andhra Pradesh, India, has an advanced case of AIDS. She is likely to die soon.

EFFECTS OF AIDS

Common problems for AIDS sufferers include:

- **skin problems, with scabs known as lesions appearing**
- **difficulty breathing**
- **finding it hard to digest food**
- **problems with the central nervous system.**

Patients with AIDS are also more likely to develop certain kinds of cancer.

HOW DO PEOPLE CATCH HIV?

Compared to many viruses, HIV is hard to catch. Once it is exposed to the air, it dies very quickly. It is passed from one person to another when their body fluids, almost always blood or semen, mix together.

A sexually transmitted disease

HIV is most often passed on when people have sex. Sadly, this means that many people have caught the virus from a person they trusted. Pissamai Trakulsanitmaitri from Thailand says:

❝ My husband was a soldier. He was away for long periods of time. He slept with a prostitute. I caught HIV from him. ❞

Pissamai's husband and her baby daughter later died of AIDS.

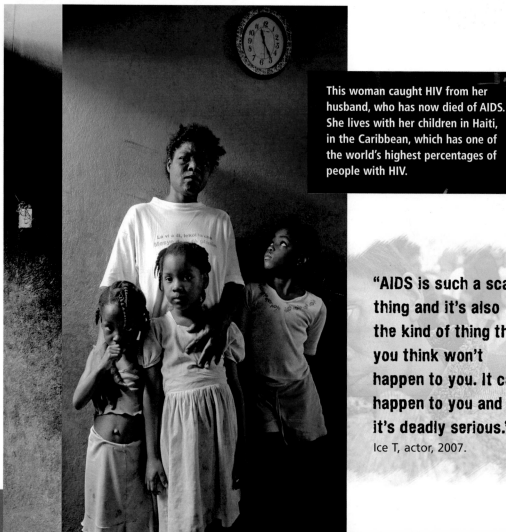

This woman caught HIV from her husband, who has now died of AIDS. She lives with her children in Haiti, in the Caribbean, which has one of the world's highest percentages of people with HIV.

"AIDS is such a scary thing and it's also the kind of thing that you think won't happen to you. It can happen to you and it's deadly serious."
Ice T, actor, 2007.

A drug user injects himself with heroin. When drug users and others share needles for injections, they risk passing on the HIV virus.

HIV/AIDS STATISTICS

- By 2007, about 25 million people had died of AIDS.

- Today, roughly 90% of people who have HIV are living in poorer countries.

- In 2007, over 2 million people died of the disease, and 2.5 million were newly infected with it.

- More than half of the adults living with HIV/AIDS are women.

UNAIDS, 2008

Needles and blood

Many people have caught HIV after using needles that have not been cleaned properly. Mindy from New York, USA says:

❝ I have been HIV positive for the past four years. I caught HIV by making the biggest mistake of my life... getting a tattoo. ❞

The needles that were used to make the tattoo still contained the blood of someone with HIV. In a similar way, drug users who share a needle to inject drugs also risk catching the virus. And some people have caught HIV after accidentally being given infected blood:

❝ My name is Ryan White. I am sixteen years old. I have haemophilia, and I have AIDS. ❞

Ryan caught HIV when he was given a blood transfusion to treat his haemophilia.

WHO IS MOST LIKELY TO CATCH HIV?

Anyone can catch HIV. Like a dose of the measles (though much more deadly), HIV isn't picky about who it infects. Some people, though, are more likely to catch the disease than others.

High-risk behaviour

Some people behave in a way that makes them more likely to come into contact with the HIV virus. Most people are passed the disease during sex, so anyone who has sex with lots of different people is more likely to catch HIV. Adam, from Los Angeles, USA remembers:

" In the early days, we didn't really know about AIDS. No one worried about having sex with people without wearing a condom. That's what helped the disease to spread so quickly. "

Drug users who inject drugs into their veins are also more likely than other people to catch HIV.

This prostitute in Cambodia is HIV positive. Because prostitutes have a lot of sexual partners, they are more likely than other people to come into contact with HIV.

AIDS IN POOR COUNTRIES

In 2007:

- Over a third (22.5 million) of all HIV/AIDS sufferers lived in sub-Saharan Africa.

- Just eight African countries accounted for a third of all new infections and a third of all AIDS deaths around the world.

- In Eastern Europe and Central Asia, the number of people with HIV/AIDS had trebled since 2001.

- The disease was spreading faster in Indonesia than anywhere else.

UNAIDS, 2008

Risk among the poor

In wealthy countries, health workers have made sure that most people know how to avoid catching HIV. But in poorer countries, people are less educated about the disease. In sub-Saharan Africa, AIDS is the biggest cause of death. Jeremy Cronin, a South African politician, once said:

❝ [The number of] Africans... dying every year of AIDS... makes the war in Iraq look like a birthday party. ❞

People with HIV are often shunned by their neighbours, or even forced to leave their communities. Sarah fled from a small village in South Africa:

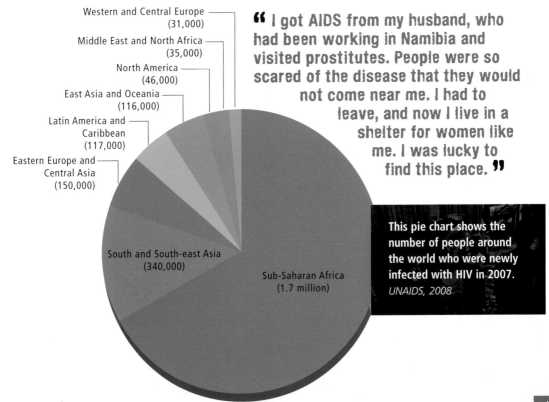

Western and Central Europe (31,000)
Middle East and North Africa (35,000)
North America (46,000)
East Asia and Oceania (116,000)
Latin America and Caribbean (117,000)
Eastern Europe and Central Asia (150,000)
South and South-east Asia (340,000)
Sub-Saharan Africa (1.7 million)

❝ I got AIDS from my husband, who had been working in Namibia and visited prostitutes. People were so scared of the disease that they would not come near me. I had to leave, and now I live in a shelter for women like me. I was lucky to find this place. ❞

This pie chart shows the number of people around the world who were newly infected with HIV in 2007.
UNAIDS, 2008

IS SAFE SEX THE ANSWER?

Safe sex is sex with a very low risk of catching HIV. It prevents HIV infection by making sure that your body fluids do not mix with someone else's.

Using a condom

For most people, 'safe sex' means sex using a condom, which stops body fluids mixing together. Many men do not like wearing a condom. As Simon said on an Internet forum:

❝ The trouble with safe sex is that condoms are horrible things that make sex less pleasant... Add that to the fact that you've got to stop what you're doing to put the thing on, and you've got a recipe for disaster! ❞

This is such a big problem that some websites give women advice on how to get men to wear a condom:

Man: ❝ It ruins the mood. ❞

Woman: ❝ Unsafe sex puts me out of the mood – for good. ❞

Condoms are readily available in most countries. Because condoms form a physical barrier between two people while they are having sex, they can prevent the spread of HIV.

HIV INFECTION

HIGH RISK	VERY SLIGHT RISK	NO RISK
Sex without a condom.	Sex with a condom.	Closed-mouth kissing.
Sharing needles for injecting drugs.	French kissing.	Touching sweat from an HIV-positive person.
	Being bitten.	

US Centers for Disease Control and Prevention

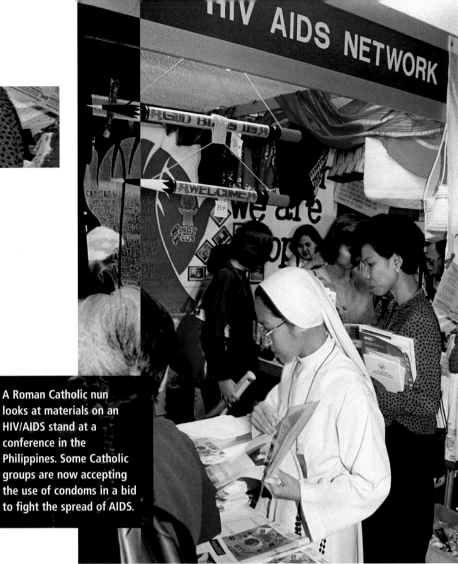

A Roman Catholic nun looks at materials on an HIV/AIDS stand at a conference in the Philippines. Some Catholic groups are now accepting the use of condoms in a bid to fight the spread of AIDS.

Objecting to safe sex

Some people object to safe sex for religious reasons. The Roman Catholic Church, for example, has told people that they should not use condoms. One Catholic wrote:

❝ The Catholic Church cannot condone, let alone sanction [approve], the use of condoms among married couples, even if one spouse has AIDS. ❞

Other people have pointed out that this policy causes much misery and suffering by denying people the protection they need.

"The Pope has swept through Africa, where 5 million people are already infected with the AIDS virus, and which expects by the end of the century to have 10 million orphans whose parents have died of AIDS – and told them not to use condoms."

Brenda Maddox, US journalist, 1990.

IS NO SEX THE ANSWER?

The only way to be sure of not catching the HIV virus through sex is to avoid having sex altogether. This is often known as abstinence.

Risky business

Some young people feel that sex is a risky business. It can expose people not only to HIV infection, but also to other STDs as well as teenage pregnancy. Many teenagers, like this girl, are deciding to wait before having sex:

❝ Sex is for adults who love each other, not for children or teenagers who think they know what love is. ❞

Millions of young people have taken what is called the Pledge:

❝ Believing that true love waits, I make a commitment to God, myself, my family, those I date, and my future mate to be sexually pure until the day I enter marriage. ❞

"There is a difference between love and sex and it is not necessary to have sex with someone to show them that you love or care about them."

'It's Great to Wait', Florida Department of Health, 2007.

These young people in the USA have decided to join the True Love Waits organisation, and have promised not to have sex until they are married.

If young people choose to have sex, it is their responsibility to make sure it is safe sex. These girls are buying condoms from a vending machine.

"A survey of more than 2,000 teenagers carried out by a research company on behalf of Congress found that the half of the sample given abstinence-only education displayed exactly the same predilection [tendency] for sex as those who had received conventional sex education in which contraception was discussed."

Quoted in *The Guardian* newspaper, 16 April 2007.

Anti-abstinence

Many young people feel they should be free to make their own decisions about sex. One teenager asked:

❝ What's wrong with being sexually active if it's with someone you absolutely love and trust more than anything or anyone? What can you see wrong with a happy, healthy sexual relationship? ❞

Another wrote:

❝ [Some people] say it's just for married couples, because I guess that's what the good ol' Bible says... I still think it's okay if you really love that person. And as long as you don't do it for the sole purpose of being able to say you aren't a virgin anymore. ❞

IS AIDS A GAY DISEASE?

HIV and AIDS first became widely known in the 1980s. In wealthy countries, it was mainly gay men who first got the virus. This led to a common belief that AIDS was a gay disease.

Mourners gather in 1987 at a memorial to AIDS victims in Washington, DC. Each square of these colourful quilts has been decorated in memory of someone who died of the disease.

Jumping to conclusions

Gay is a word used to describe people who are homosexual, or attracted to people of their own sex. In the early days of AIDS, many people judged gays unfairly and even held them responsible for the disease. One gay man remembers the misery this caused for sufferers:

❝ The ones who died early on created the most heart-wrenching times for us, because they were subjected to the worst kinds of fear and isolation, even by those who were supposed to be providing their medical care. Many doctors and nurses refused to give even the minimal comfort that was available at the time, and many family and friends [did not give] their support and love, as well. ❞

Battling against prejudice

Slowly, people began to understand that HIV could be caught in lots of ways, by anyone, and wasn't just a gay disease. Many haemophiliacs – who need regular blood transfusions – were given infected blood without anyone realising. But people still held prejudices against HIV and AIDS. TJ, from the USA, describes his father's battle:

❝ My dad was a haemophiliac who contracted HIV/AIDS through the blood products that he used to stop his bleeding... When he disclosed it to his co-workers he was treated like a leper. Our neighbour was so afraid of him, she had to get counselling...

My dad lived with HIV/AIDS for 12 years, and his mission was to educate people that they needn't be afraid of him. In fact, he was more afraid of them – afraid of catching colds or infections from them that could literally kill him. He passed away in 1998. ❞

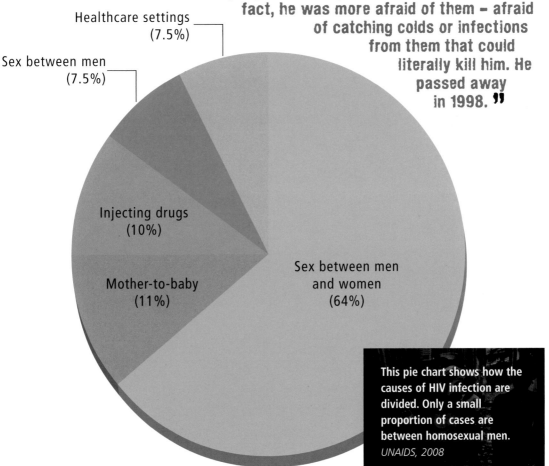

Healthcare settings
(7.5%)

Sex between men
(7.5%)

Injecting drugs
(10%)

Mother-to-baby
(11%)

Sex between men
and women
(64%)

This pie chart shows how the causes of HIV infection are divided. Only a small proportion of cases are between homosexual men.
UNAIDS, 2008

"We've said for a long time... that if you do engage in risky activities you run the risk of getting [HIV], and that it really has little to do with your sexual preferences."
AIDS activist Jerry Thacker, 2008.

IS AIDS GOD'S JUDGEMENT?

HIV can be caught only through certain acts. Some religious people believe that these acts, in particular gay sex and injecting drugs, are unacceptable. They suggest that HIV is God's way of telling people that their behaviour is wrong.

A sinful life

A few campaigners have suggested that HIV is the result of people leading what they see as a sinful life. The British campaigner Mary Whitehouse, for example, once claimed that:

❝ AIDS is a judgment we have brought upon ourselves. ❞

In the USA, the Christian preacher Reverend Jerry Falwell once said:

❝ AIDS is not just God's punishment for homosexuals; it is God's punishment for the society that tolerates homosexuals. ❞

To some people who hold similar views, drug users, homosexual men, and the promiscuous catch HIV as a punishment for their behaviour.

'Fags' is American slang for homosexual men. This man has an extreme view that AIDS stops the 'disease' of homosexuality by killing gay people.

An equal-opportunities disease

Many people disagree with the idea that HIV/AIDS is a punishment from God. They argue that millions of people who could not be said to deserve HIV have caught it, including haemophiliacs and children. One woman on an Internet forum for mothers said:

❝ My baby got HIV from my breast milk. I may have done some stupid things in my life, and behaved badly, but that little baby hadn't hurt a soul. When I hear preachers saying that AIDS is God's judgment – well, it makes me mad. ❞

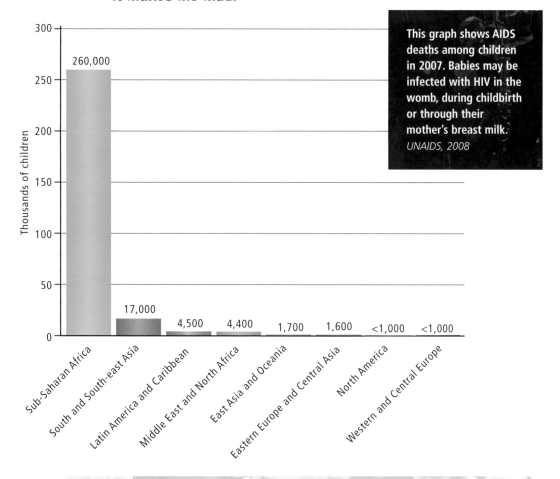

This graph shows AIDS deaths among children in 2007. Babies may be infected with HIV in the womb, during childbirth or through their mother's breast milk.
UNAIDS, 2008

Thousands of children

- Sub-Saharan Africa: 260,000
- South and South-east Asia: 17,000
- Latin America and Caribbean: 4,500
- Middle East and North Africa: 4,400
- East Asia and Oceania: 1,700
- Eastern Europe and Central Asia: 1,600
- North America: <1,000
- Western and Central Europe: <1,000

"Religious communities, mosques, temples [and] churches... have reached out to provide support to those living with and affected by HIV. Their leadership has great influence in the lives of many people, and leaders speaking out responsibly about AIDS can make a powerful impact at both community and international level."

UNAIDS statement, 2008.

IS AIDS THE PLANET'S REVENGE?

The world's population is increasing rapidly. By 2025, there will probably be 25 per cent more people than there are today. Could HIV/AIDS be nature's way of keeping human numbers down?

Millions of people flock every day to this market in Lagos, Nigeria. Lagos is one of a growing number of world 'megacities', with more than 10 million inhabitants.

Resource-hungry people

Many people think that the planet cannot cope with the demands of the current population. Many resources are running low, and we find it harder and harder to grow enough food for everyone. Some people have suggested that diseases do a good job of stopping our population from increasing too much. As the undersea explorer Jacques Cousteau argued:

❝ It's a wonderful idea [to eliminate suffering and disease] but perhaps not altogether a beneficial one in the long run... World population must be stabilised, and to do that we [would] need to eliminate 350,000 people per day. ❞

The numbers don't add up

Other people have noted that, if HIV is meant to be some sort of design for stopping population increase, it probably won't work very well. According to one writer in an Internet article:

> **The idea that AIDS will solve the population explosion does not stand up to reason. About 200 million people in Africa will be HIV infected by 2010, but the loss of 200 million people would not slow population growth. The fourteenth century's Black Death killed more than 50 per cent of the European population, but by 1750 Europe had reached the population size it would have reached without the Black Death.**

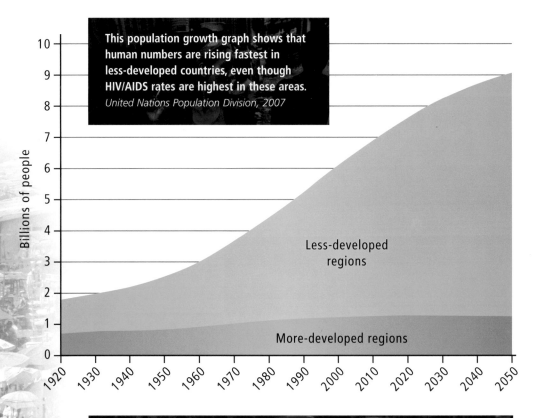

This population growth graph shows that human numbers are rising fastest in less-developed countries, even though HIV/AIDS rates are highest in these areas.
United Nations Population Division, 2007

Less-developed regions

More-developed regions

Billions of people

GLOBAL STATISTICS SNAPSHOT

- **Daily population increase in 2007:**   212,036
- **Total population increase in 2007:**   77.4 million
- **AIDS deaths in 2007:**   2 million.

UNAIDS, GeoHive

WHAT HELPED AIDS TO INCREASE IN POORER COUNTRIES?

Today, roughly nine out of every ten people with HIV/AIDS live in one of the world's poorer countries. The disease affects southern Africa worst. Why has HIV become such a problem for the poor?

Rich losing interest

Some people feel that rich countries have not done enough to halt the spread of AIDS in poorer parts of the world. They say that richer countries have lost interest in the dangers of HIV – both at home and abroad. According to Michael Merson, former Director of the World Health Organisation's AIDS programme:

❝ In the 90s it became clear we were not going to have a major heterosexual epidemic in the States. [AIDS] was no longer a threat to the West. ❞

Because of this, wealthy Western governments were no longer as interested in educating people to fight the disease worldwide.

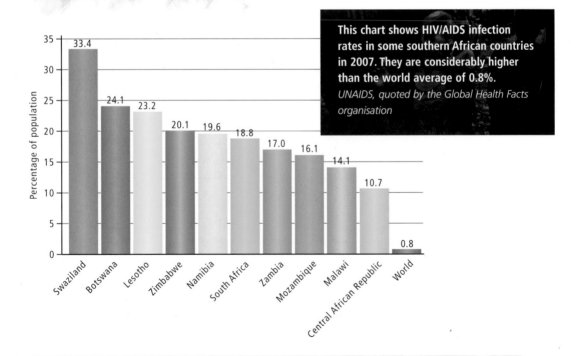

This chart shows HIV/AIDS infection rates in some southern African countries in 2007. They are considerably higher than the world average of 0.8%.
UNAIDS, quoted by the Global Health Facts organisation

Percentage of population

Country	%
Swaziland	33.4
Botswana	24.1
Lesotho	23.2
Zimbabwe	20.1
Namibia	19.6
South Africa	18.8
Zambia	17.0
Mozambique	16.1
Malawi	14.1
Central African Republic	10.7
World	0.8

"When the rich lose their fear, they are not willing to invest in the problems of the poor."

Dr William Foege, the former Director of the US Centers for Disease Control and Prevention.

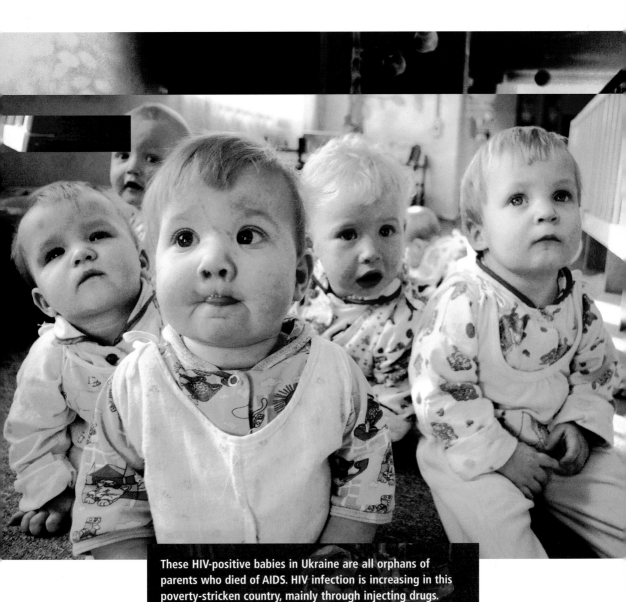

These HIV-positive babies in Ukraine are all orphans of parents who died of AIDS. HIV infection is increasing in this poverty-stricken country, mainly through injecting drugs.

Old habits die hard

Some observers argue that HIV has spread in poorer countries because people there have not changed their behaviour in order to stay safe. Injecting drugs using shared needles is an increasing problem on the streets. And too many men still have many sexual partners and refuse to wear a condom, even though they know the risks. As Fon, from Thailand, says:

❝ I work as a prostitute in Bangkok. We get tested for diseases regularly, but the men who come here often refuse to wear a condom. Every time we have sex with them, we risk getting HIV. Now some of the girls I know have the virus. Some are still working, so they are spreading the disease to anyone who won't wear a condom. Sometimes I think this is justice. ❞

CAN MALE CIRCUMCISION PREVENT AIDS?

In 2006, a trial showed that HIV/AIDS rates were relatively low among men who had been circumcised. Men with no foreskin seemed to be only half as likely to catch the virus. Could circumcision help to beat the threat of AIDS?

Circumcision and HIV

In Africa and Asia, the countries where men are commonly circumcised are the countries where HIV infection rates are low. Where men are not circumcised, infection rates are higher. However, many men do not want to be circumcised. Moses, from Kenya, claims:

" This is a part of what makes me a man. Why should I have a piece of my manhood cut away? Also, not having a foreskin makes sex less good – and who wants that? "

INFECTION V. FORESKINS

In sub-Saharan Africa:

● Countries where less than 20% of men have been circumcised have an average HIV infection rate of 18.8%.

● Countries where over 80% of men have been circumcised have an average infection rate of 4.6%.

World Health Organisation, 2006

Boys of the Mbuti tribe dance at their circumcision ceremony in the Democratic Republic of Congo. Regions where circumcision is common usually have lower rates of HIV infection than places where it is not.

Not a fail-safe measure

Being circumcised seems to make a man less likely to catch HIV, but it is still possible to catch the disease even without a foreskin. It would be dangerous for men to think that because they are circumcised, they are safe from the HIV virus. Tom, who works for an AIDS charity, explains:

❝ There is a real danger in sending out a message that circumcision can protect against HIV. This is not the case and could lead to an increase in unprotected sex... [Condoms] are the most effective method currently available for preventing HIV. ❞

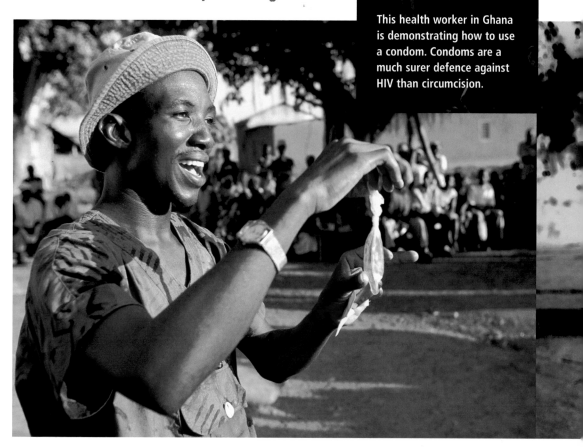

This health worker in Ghana is demonstrating how to use a condom. Condoms are a much surer defence against HIV than circumcision.

"Male circumcision reduces the risk of HIV infection, but it only provides partial protection. Circumcised men are not immune to the virus. Male circumcision must not be promoted alone, but alongside other methods to reduce the risk of HIV – including avoidance of unsafe sexual practices, reduction in the number of sexual partners, and correct and consistent condom use."
World Health Organisation report, 2007.

SHOULD EVERYONE BE TESTED?

It isn't possible to tell by looking at someone whether they have the HIV virus or not. Some people have the disease without knowing it. So, should everyone be tested for HIV?

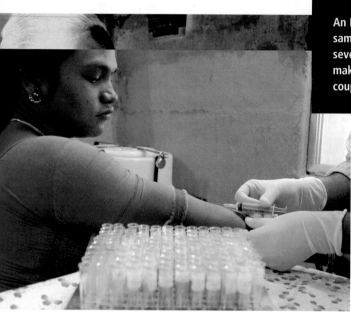

An Indian woman gives a blood sample to be tested for HIV. In 2008, several Indian states proposed to make HIV tests compulsory for couples wanting to get married.

Test is best

If everyone knew whether they had the HIV virus or not, they could change the way they acted accordingly. They could have safe sex, or no sex, so that there was no risk of passing the virus to someone else. Jaya, from India, thinks that everyone should have an HIV test before they get married:

MANDATORY TESTING

Over 50 countries require foreigners who want to go and live in them to take an HIV test. They include:

● Australia

● Canada

● China (except for Hong Kong and Macau)

● India.

" [I] do not care what people do in their personal lives and [do not want] to intrude on their space. However, there are an increasing number of cases where a person does not know, or deliberately hides, his or her HIV status and goes ahead with an arranged marriage. The spouse and the children are [then] at high risk and bear the brunt of it all their lives. "

This woman in Swaziland knew that she had the HIV virus before she became pregnant. Without modern drugs to prevent it, many HIV mothers pass the virus on to their children.

"HIV testing without informed consent and confidentiality is a violation of human rights. Moreover, there is no evidence that mandatory testing achieves public health goals. UNAIDS therefore discourages this practice."
United Nations policy document, 1997.

Knowledge isn't everything

Even when people know that they have HIV, it does not always make a difference to how they behave. Sarita from Mumbai, in India, says:

❝ My husband never told me [that he had HIV], and died as an outcast AIDS patient in a local hospital... After he was admitted I was told to go for tests, and the doctors discovered that I had contracted [HIV] too. Over the last few years I have lost family support and I cannot work like before. I was cheated and the person who cheated me is dead. I wish things had been different. ❞

Making Sarita's husband have an HIV test would not have made a difference – he DID have a test, but chose not to tell her that he had HIV.

SHOULD PEOPLE KEEP THE DISEASE SECRET?

People who have HIV may not show any sign of being unwell. Unless they reveal that they have the virus, no one will know. But should people be allowed to keep the fact that they have HIV secret?

Would these people still be dancing so close together if one of them had just announced that he or she had HIV?

Risks to others

Some people feel that those who have HIV should let others know. That way, they can decide exactly how they want to relate to the person who has HIV. Jan, from Stockholm in Sweden, argues:

❝ I think if someone knows they have HIV, they should tell people about it. If I knew one of my friends had the bug, I'd be much more careful about touching him or things he'd touched, or eating with him – stuff like that. ❞

In fact, it would be practically impossible to catch HIV from someone by touching something they had touched, or by eating with them.

"Most people agree that privacy for [HIV] patients should be respected, but at the same time they find it difficult to accept that an anonymous HIV carrier could be their colleague or neighbour."
Article in China's *People's Daily* newspaper, 2002.

> **"Rampant discrimination, which inhibits people from voluntarily seeking advice and the testing of possible HIV carriers, is a major reason for the rapidly increasing spread of AIDS in China."**
>
> Director of UNAIDS, China, quoted in Chinese *People's Daily* in 2002.

Risk of being shunned

Because many people do not understand HIV and how it is passed on, some think it is best not to admit having the disease. Aña, from Haiti, reasons:

> **❝ No normal person would deliberately give another person HIV. I make sure I don't risk other people catching the disease. But if you tell others, you end up being treated differently, as if you were some kind of poison. ❞**

One man in South Africa remembered the effects of knowing that someone had HIV:

> **❝ An acquaintance confided that she had HIV. Later she flirted with a friend of mine who did not know her status. Should I have tipped him off – or respected the confidence and trusted her to tell him herself? I tipped him off and he fled. She felt betrayed. ❞**

An AIDS sufferer in China lies on his deathbed, alongside his two children. The family has been forced to live apart from other people, because no one wants them nearby.

CAN AIDS BE TREATED?

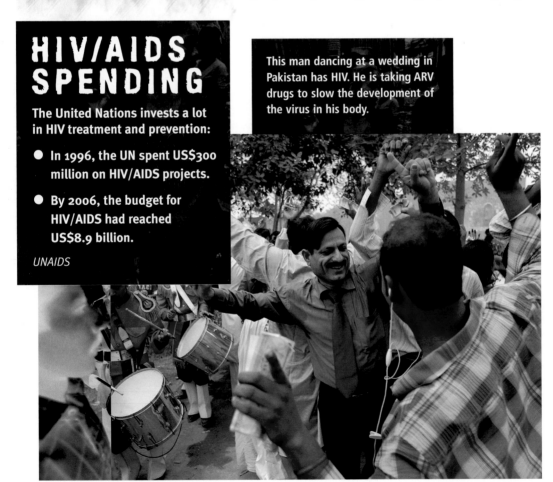

There is still no cure for the HIV virus. But over the last ten years, drugs called antiretrovirals have become available. These make patients' immune systems stronger, and help them to resist the effects of HIV.

A new lease on life

Antiretrovirals (often called ARVs) can give many people who have HIV a new lease on life. Taking the drugs can allow them to work and live independently for many years. Thembela, from South Africa, was so sure she was about to die from HIV infection that she gave away all her clothes. Now – five years later – she says:

" We don't talk about death much these days, since I started taking [antiretrovirals]. The drugs have made me stronger, and now I am more worried about whether my boyfriend can find a job, and putting on weight, than dying. "

HIV/AIDS SPENDING

The United Nations invests a lot in HIV treatment and prevention:

- In 1996, the UN spent US$300 million on HIV/AIDS projects.

- By 2006, the budget for HIV/AIDS had reached US$8.9 billion.

UNAIDS

This man dancing at a wedding in Pakistan has HIV. He is taking ARV drugs to slow the development of the virus in his body.

An HIV patient sits with the selection of drugs that he has to take every single day. Some of the drugs have unpleasant side effects.

Not for everyone

ARVs don't work for everyone. Some people feel very sick when taking them, as Adam from Sydney, Australia remembers:

" In my second year on ARVs, I started feeling sick. I had stomach aches and my buttocks got smaller... I had to change my medication. [But] I am feeling well now on the new treatment. "

The ARVs are usually a cocktail of different drugs. Some patients find it impossible to settle on a combination that carries on working for them. Allan, from Denmark, explains:

" I have a whole kitchen cabinet full of drugs, and I have to take pills every few hours. Every year or so I have to change the combination of drugs I take. My doctor says that soon we're going to run out of combinations. "

HAVE ATTITUDES TO HIV CHANGED?

Because antiretroviral drugs work so well, some people have started to take HIV infection less seriously. Are they right to treat HIV infection in this way?

Changing views

In the 1980s and 1990s, when HIV/AIDS first appeared, the virus caused great fear. Governments launched 'safe sex' campaigns, to let people know the dangers of the disease. Greg, writing on an Internet forum in 2008, has noticed a change in attitude:

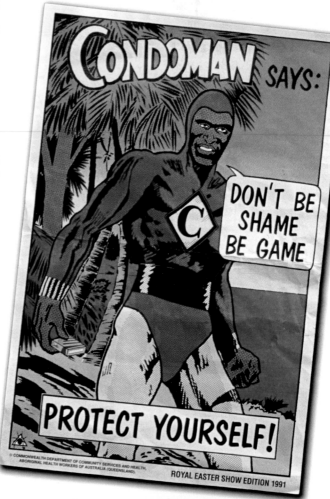

❝ I'm 32 years old and remember getting the safe sex message pushed hard at me in the 90s. The younger guys at work... are out on the pull with a different girl every week, completely unaware of the risks. ❞

These people risk catching HIV because they haven't taken the dangers of the disease seriously.

Condoman says, 'Protect Yourself!' in this 1991 HIV/AIDS public health campaign from Australia.

"Of about 19 million new STD infections in the USA each year, almost half are recorded among people aged 15 to 24."
Article in *The Guardian* newspaper, 2007.

"The number of new HIV infections in men under 30 who have sex with men has increased sharply in New York City in the last five years... even as AIDS deaths and overall HIV infection rates in the city have steadily declined."

New York Times, 2 January 2008.

Bug chasers

Almost everyone catches HIV by accident. But recently some gay men seem to have decided to catch HIV on purpose. They are known as 'bug chasers'. One man in his 20s, from Melbourne, Australia, said:

❝ There were parts of me, dark corners, that wanted it, that were thinking, 'Let's just do it and get it over and done with and then it won't be an issue'. ❞

However, not everyone is convinced that bug chasers really exist. Mike Kennedy of the Victorian AIDS Council, Australia, is doubtful:

❝ You will find one of everything you look for, but the notion that this is a big scene, absolutely not. The [idea] of 'bug chasers' – it's something that's come off the Internet. ❞

Partygoers relax at a gay club in Paris, France. Most people find the attitude of bug chasers hard to understand – not everyone agrees that they even exist.

HAVE ARVS SLOWED THE SPREAD OF HIV?

Antiretroviral drugs have helped to slow the number of deaths from HIV/AIDS. But have these expensive drugs really done anything to prevent the spread of the disease itself?

A profitable business

Some campaigners have pointed out that while ARVs provide some relief for patients, they don't actually cure the HIV virus or stop it from spreading. They do, however, make billions of dollars a year for the drugs companies that manufacture them. As Barbara, a US activist, said:

❝ From the point of view of the pharmaceutical industry, the AIDS problem has already been solved. After all, we already have a drug which can be sold at the incredible price of US$8,000 an annual dose, and which has the added virtue of not diminishing the market by actually curing anyone. ❞

This graph shows the number of people living with HIV between 1990 and 2007. The figures have increased, despite advances in ARV treatment.
UNAIDS, 2008

ARVS IN NUMBERS

In 2004, the global market for ARVs was estimated to be worth US$6.6 billion.

LeadDiscovery, 2005

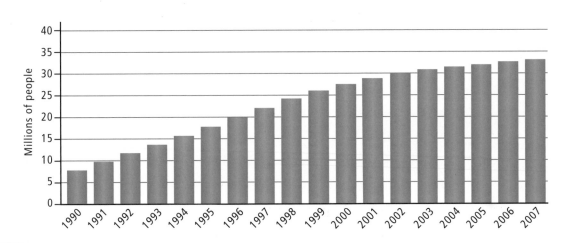

Millions of people

| 1990 | 1991 | 1992 | 1993 | 1994 | 1995 | 1996 | 1997 | 1998 | 1999 | 2000 | 2001 | 2002 | 2003 | 2004 | 2005 | 2006 | 2007 |

Making the problem worse

In fact, some people argue that ARVs may increase the spread of HIV because they make people take the threat of the disease less seriously. One man, interviewed in an Australian newspaper, commented that catching the virus now that drugs are available:

❝ Wouldn't be as catastrophic as it might have been ten years ago. ❞

The same problem exists all round the world. A doctor working in Botswana wrote:

❝ It has been my experience that some people in Botswana are beginning to view ARVs as a safety net; [they think that] risky behaviour is OK because there are ARVs. ❞

A health worker holds up a poster showing an AIDS patient before (left) and after ARV treatment. Do promotions like this make people think ARVs are a miracle cure?

"The perceptions of the negative aspects of HIV infection have been minimised since the introduction of [ARVs], which has led to a false understanding of what living with HIV means and thus to an increase in risky sexual behaviours."

US Centers for Disease Control and Prevention, 2005.

SHOULD AIDS DRUGS BE CHEAPER?

Drugs to treat HIV/AIDS are expensive, and are produced by big international companies that exist to make money. Are the drugs companies profiting at a cost to the sick?

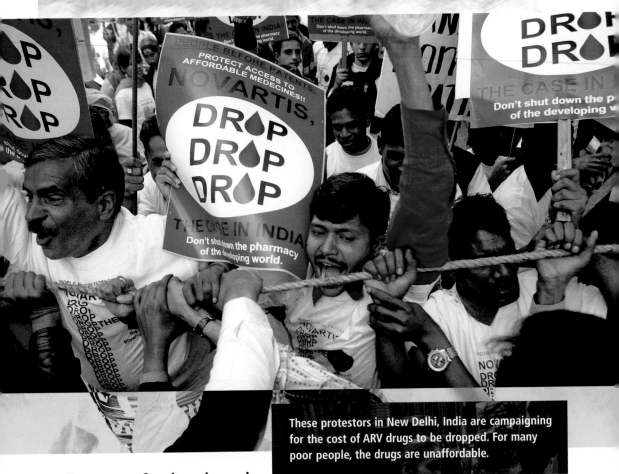

These protestors in New Delhi, India are campaigning for the cost of ARV drugs to be dropped. For many poor people, the drugs are unaffordable.

Too poor for treatment

Antiretrovirals were developed by companies that hold patents for the drugs. This means that the drugs cannot be made by someone else unless they pay the drugs company a fee. In the past, this made ARVs too expensive for poor people. As Maria, from Brooklyn, USA, said:

❝ I caught HIV in 2004, from a shared needle. I can't afford all the drugs I should take, and now my blood tests say that the HIV is getting worse. Soon, the doctor thinks I'll have full-blown AIDS. ❞

Beyond cost

Recently, many drugs companies have agreed to reduce the cost of their HIV drugs in poor countries. Even this, though, may not mean that the drugs get to the people who need them. As Sophie, from Harare in Zimbabwe, said:

" Even now, most people can't afford antiretrovirals... Our government is in the process of setting up antiretroviral programmes but things are taking a while to happen. We do not have enough doctors and setting up a programme like this takes time and resources that we do not currently have. "

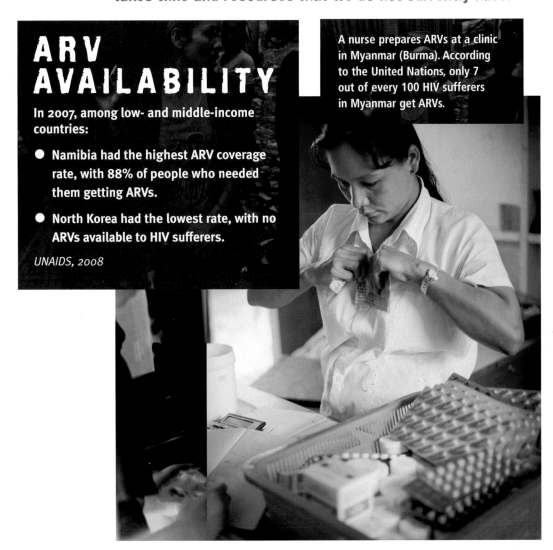

ARV AVAILABILITY

In 2007, among low- and middle-income countries:

● Namibia had the highest ARV coverage rate, with 88% of people who needed them getting ARVs.

● North Korea had the lowest rate, with no ARVs available to HIV sufferers.

UNAIDS, 2008

A nurse prepares ARVs at a clinic in Myanmar (Burma). According to the United Nations, only 7 out of every 100 HIV sufferers in Myanmar get ARVs.

"We need to be clear, no matter how cheap the drugs, most poor people will not receive them because there is no health system that reaches them."
Clare Short, former UK International Development Secretary, 2003.

COULD GOVERNMENTS DO MORE?

Governments around the world have very different attitudes to HIV/AIDS. Some plough money into helping victims of the disease. Others come close to denying it even exists.

Against ARVs

The South African government has one of the worst records in the world for fighting HIV. Some of its leaders have opposed the use of ARVs, declaring that they are pointless or even dangerous. Peter Mokaba, a politician who is said later to have died of AIDS, once announced:

" Antiretrovirals, they're... poison actually. We cannot allow our people to take something so dangerous that it will actually exterminate them. However well meaning, the hazards of misplaced compassion could lead to genocide. "

ARV NEED IN SOUTH AFRICA

In 2007, between 1.5 and 1.8 million South Africans were estimated to be in need of ARVs. Only 28% were receiving them.

UNAIDS, quoted by Global Health Facts, 2008

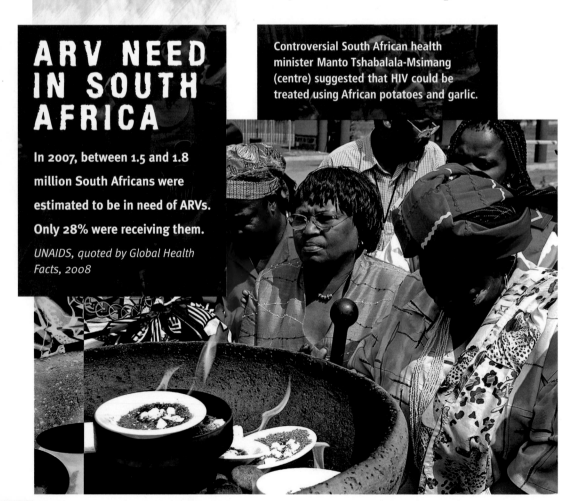

Controversial South African health minister Manto Tshabalala-Msimang (centre) suggested that HIV could be treated using African potatoes and garlic.

"[South Africa] is the only country in Africa whose government continues to propound [propose] theories more worthy of a lunatic fringe than of a concerned and compassionate state."

Stephen Lewis, UN special envoy to Africa.

These HIV-positive South Africans are wearing T-shirts to encourage openness about HIV. They are part of a World AIDS Day campaign to improve treatment and support for AIDS sufferers.

Set a better example

Few people who have taken ARVs agree that they are harmful. Lala from Zimbabwe believes that governments should encourage, not warn against, HIV drugs:

❝ At first I was terrified to start treatment. I had heard and read so many bad things about side effects and toxicity... [For two weeks] I felt really sick because my body was not used to the medication, but as time went on I felt totally normal, and now I feel very strong and healthy. ❞

For many people, governments also need to do more to reduce the shame attached to HIV. This young Ugandan woman hopes for a more open approach in future:

❝ When I die, people must not hide it if I died from AIDS... They must wear those T-shirts that say 'HIV Positive', and talk about how I used to love to dance. ❞

WILL AIDS EVER BE ERADICATED?

At the moment there is no cure for HIV/AIDS. Antiretrovirals can slow the disease down, but once you've got it, you can't get rid of it. Will a cure for HIV ever be found?

A cure for HIV?

Some HIV patients feel that not enough is being done to find a cure for the disease. One man posting on an Internet message board asked:

❝ Where did our fight for the cure go? I don't know when it happened or where it happened or how it happened. But we seem to have lost the fight for the cure. Have we decided to accept living taking pills, day after day, with no end in sight? Have we decided to tolerate side effects as part of our normal life? Over the last five years I have had to take at least ten pills a day. That's 18,250 pills, minimum. When do we start fighting for the cure again? ❞

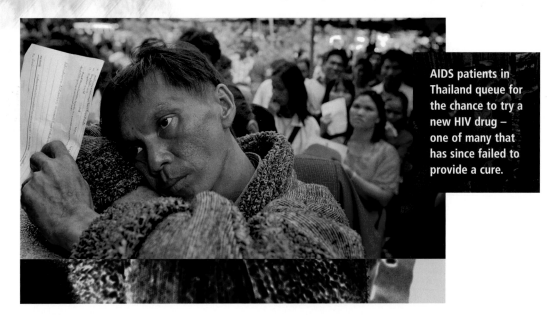

AIDS patients in Thailand queue for the chance to try a new HIV drug – one of many that has since failed to provide a cure.

"Over the past 20 years, AIDS has become a part of life everywhere on the planet [and] it remains one of the most feared of all infections... Despite medical advances, a cure is elusive. AIDS is a serious, difficult-to-treat and ultimately fatal disease."
Article in the US Food and Drug Administration magazine, *Consumer*, November 2001.

"Across the world the global epidemic of HIV/AIDS has shown itself capable of triggering responses of compassion, solidarity and support, bringing out the best in people, their families and communities. But the disease is also associated with stigma, repression and discrimination."

AVERT, an international AIDS charity.

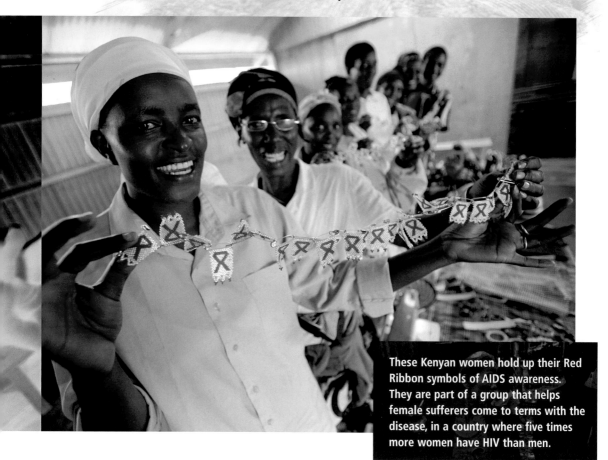

These Kenyan women hold up their Red Ribbon symbols of AIDS awareness. They are part of a group that helps female sufferers come to terms with the disease, in a country where five times more women have HIV than men.

Is a cure the point?

Finding a cure for AIDS is easier said than done. Scientists are working hard to try to conquer the virus, but any new drugs must go through lengthy and expensive trials. Even then, there is no guarantee that they will succeed. Preventing the spread of HIV remains vitally important. In the meantime, people like Annabel from Zimbabwe, are focusing on managing their disease:

❝ Knowing my status helped me to take action and be proactive. Most people see HIV as a death sentence. It was my Wake-Up Call! We don't always realise the value of life until it is threatened, so remember to always respect, protect and love yourself and your body. Every time I find myself getting down about life I remind myself that today I am healthy and well, and I can live for today! ❞

TIMELINE

1930s   Researchers think that some time in the 1930s, a virus that became HIV-1 jumped from apes to humans in Africa.

1950s   The first AIDS deaths probably occur, though the evidence is not certain.

1960s   A second virus, HIV-2, is thought to have jumped from monkeys to people.

1966   In about 1966, the HIV virus is thought to have spread from Africa to the USA. In 1969, a teenager in St Louis, USA dies of what is later discovered to be AIDS.

1970s   Norwegian, Danish, American and Portuguese citizens die of what is later confirmed as being HIV/AIDS.

5 June 1981   A study of an unusual cluster of pneumonia cases among gay men in the USA alerts the world to AIDS. By the end of the year, 121 people are known to have died from the disease. The UK's first case is confirmed.

1982   AIDS (Acquired Immune Deficiency Syndrome) is first used as a term. The condition had earlier been known as GRID (Gay Related Immune Deficiency).

1982   The first case of AIDS is reported in Africa. A baby in California, USA becomes the first person known to be infected through a blood transfusion.

1983   The US Centers for Disease Control and Prevention add female partners to the list of groups at risk. The HIV virus is identified by scientists for the first time.

1984   HIV (Human Immunodeficiency Virus) is isolated by Luc Montagnier of the Pasteur Institute in Paris and Robert Gallo of the US National Cancer Institute.

1985   Hollywood star Rock Hudson is revealed to have AIDS, and dies on 2 October.

1987   AZT, the first antiretroviral drug, becomes available.

1987   The UK government launches a 'Don't Die of Ignorance' campaign. Needle exchanges for drug users are first trialled in the UK.

1987   Pictures of Princess Diana holding the hand of a patient in an AIDS ward are broadcast around the world.

1988 The first World AIDS Day takes place.

1991 Freddie Mercury, lead singer of Queen, dies of an AIDS-related illness, as does US actor Anthony Perkins. Basketball star Magic Johnson announces that he is HIV positive.

1991 The Red Ribbon becomes the international symbol of HIV.

1991 The US Food and Drug Administration licenses the first rapid HIV test.

1991 Ten million people around the world are HIV positive. AIDS kills more men aged 25 to 44 than any other condition.

1995 There is an outbreak of HIV among injecting drug users in Eastern Europe.

1995 The first combination therapy – HAART (Highly Active Antiretroviral Therapy) is approved for use in the USA.

1996 UNAIDS, the United Nations organisation for monitoring and fighting AIDS, is established.

1998 Trials of a vaccine against HIV begin.

2001 Drug companies abandon their opposition to the production of unbranded antiretrovirals, making it easier for poorer countries to provide ARVs to their citizens.

2002 The Global Fund for the fight against HIV/AIDS, malaria and TB is set up.

2003 Results of the first major HIV vaccine trial – Aids VAX – show promise.

2005 International leaders commit to universal access to HIV/AIDS treatment at the G8 Summit in Gleneagles, Scotland.

2005 About 1.3 million people in developing countries have access to treatment.

2005 A highly resistant strain of HIV, which rapidly develops into AIDS, is identified in New York City, USA.

2007 About 33 million people are estimated to be living with AIDS worldwide.

GLOSSARY

abstinence Going without something. Abstinence is often used to describe refraining from sexual activity.

AIDS The final, deadly stage of an infection with the HIV virus. In this final stage, the body becomes unable to defend itself against diseases, and eventually the patient dies.

blood transfusion The replacement of a person's blood, using new blood that has come from someone else.

circumcision A procedure to remove the foreskin from a man's penis.

Food and Drug Administration (FDA) The government body that oversees food and drug safety in the USA.

foreskin The loose piece of skin that surrounds the tip of the penis.

genocide The mass murder of a whole group of people because of their culture or nationality.

haemophilia A blood disease that means the blood does not clot and seal up a wound.

haemophiliac A person suffering from haemophilia. Without treatment, haemophiliacs risk bleeding to death if they are badly injured.

heterosexual Sexually attracted to people of the opposite sex.

homosexual Sexually attracted to people of your own sex.

infect To pass on an illness.

inhibits Stops or prevents.

mandatory Compulsory, describing something that you have to do.

patents Legal ways of protecting an invention from being copied. If anyone copies a patented invention, such as a new drug, without permission, they can be taken to court.

prejudice An unfair judgement or opinion, formed without knowledge of the facts.

promiscuous Likely to have sex with a lot of different people.

prostitute A person who has sex with someone for money.

resources Goods, raw materials, money and services used by people to achieve a goal.

semen Fluid that comes from a male's penis during sex.

spouse A husband or wife.

STD Sexually Transmitted Disease. HIV/AIDS can be caught as an STD.

toxicity The level of poison in something. A drug with a high level of toxicity is very poisonous.

United Nations (UN) An international organisation with over 190 member countries, which was formed in 1945 to promote world peace, good health and economic development.

violation A crime or breaking of a rule.

virus A microscopic organism (germ) that causes disease and makes copies of itself inside the body's cells.

RESOURCES

Books

HIV and AIDS (Need to Know) by Sean Connolly (Heinemann Library, 2002)

AIDS and HIV: The Facts For Kids by Rae Simons (Alpha House, 2008)

Inside AIDS: HIV Attacks The Immune System by Conrad J Storad (Lerner Publications, 1998)

Ana's Story: A Journey of Hope by Jenna Bush and Mia Baxter (HarperCollins, 2007)

Movies

Philadelphia directed by Jonathan Demme (1993)
This film stars Tom Hanks as an HIV sufferer who is fired from his job at a Philadelphia law firm, and Denzel Washington as the lawyer who helps him fight against the decision. The movie is a good way to see what life was like for many people who became HIV positive in the 1980s and 1990s.

The Ryan White Story directed by John Herzfeld (1989)
This TV movie tells the tale of Ryan White, a teenage haemophiliac who was expelled from his school when he caught the HIV virus, and whose family fought against the decision.

Websites

http://www.unaids.org
The website of UNAIDS, the United Nations organisation that coordinates the global fight against HIV and AIDS. This is a giant site: a good place to start is by clicking on the 'Knowledge Centre' heading and scrolling down to 'Fast Facts About AIDS'.

http://www.cdc.gov/hiv
The Centers for Disease Control is a US organisation interested in public health. It has a large section on HIV/AIDS, including useful pages on basic information, frequently asked questions, and global HIV/AIDS, as well as specific information about HIV in the USA.

http://www.who.int/hiv/en
The World Heath Organisation's home page on HIV/AIDS, which leads to information on a wide variety of topics and fact sheets. The site also contains region-by-region and country-by-country information.

http://www.nhs.uk/Conditions/HIV/Pages/Introduction.aspx?url=Pages/What-is-it.aspx
This page leads on to an excellent, clear set of articles by the British National Health Service on HIV/AIDS. Although the site is British, all the information about the disease is relevant around the world.

INDEX